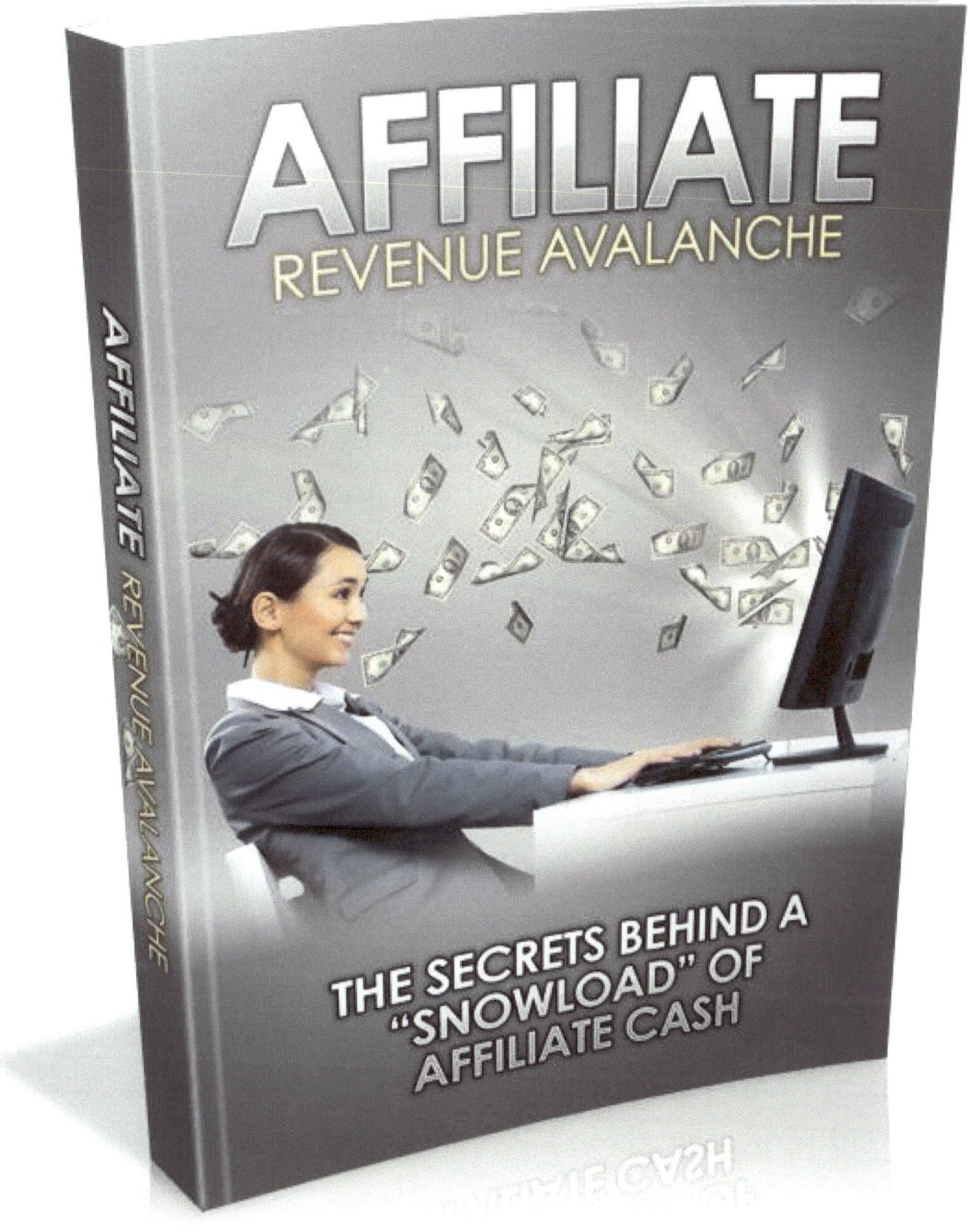
AFFILIATE
REVENUE AVALANCHE
THE SECRETS BEHIND A "SNOWLOAD" OF AFFILIATE CASH
AFFILIATE REVENUE AVALANCHE

Terms and Conditions

LEGAL NOTICE

The Publisher has strived to be as accurate and complete as possible in the creation of this report, notwithstanding the fact that he does not warrant or represent at any time that the contents within are accurate due to the rapidly changing nature of the Internet.

While all attempts have been made to verify information provided in this publication, the Publisher assumes no responsibility for errors, omissions, or contrary interpretation of the subject matter herein. Any perceived slights of specific persons, peoples, or organizations are unintentional.

In practical advice books, like anything else in life, there are no guarantees of income made. Readers are cautioned to reply on their own judgment about their individual circumstances to act accordingly.

This book is not intended for use as a source of legal, business, accounting or financial advice. All readers are advised to seek services of competent professionals in legal, business, accounting and finance fields.

You are encouraged to print this book for easy reading.

Table Of Contents

Foreword

Chapter 1:
Affiliate Basics

Chapter 2:
Anticipate The Needs Of Your Market

Chapter 3:
Supply Helpful Info About Affiliate Products You Promote

Chapter 4:
Be Truthful With Your Customers And Subscribers

Chapter 5:
Research Offers And Test Them First

Chapter 6:
Learn How To Be Patient

Wrapping Up

Foreword

Affiliate programs are now very much part and parcel of any online business endeavors. With almost every company offering some form of affiliates one would be able to understand just how much it can positively contribute to the added revenue element of the endeavor. Get all the info you need here.

Affiliate Revenue Avalanche
The Secrets Behind A "Snowload" Of Affiliate Cash

Chapter 1:
Affiliate Basics

Synopsis

As there are several types of affiliates the individual should take the time to understand the benefits of the various types before and informed decision is made.

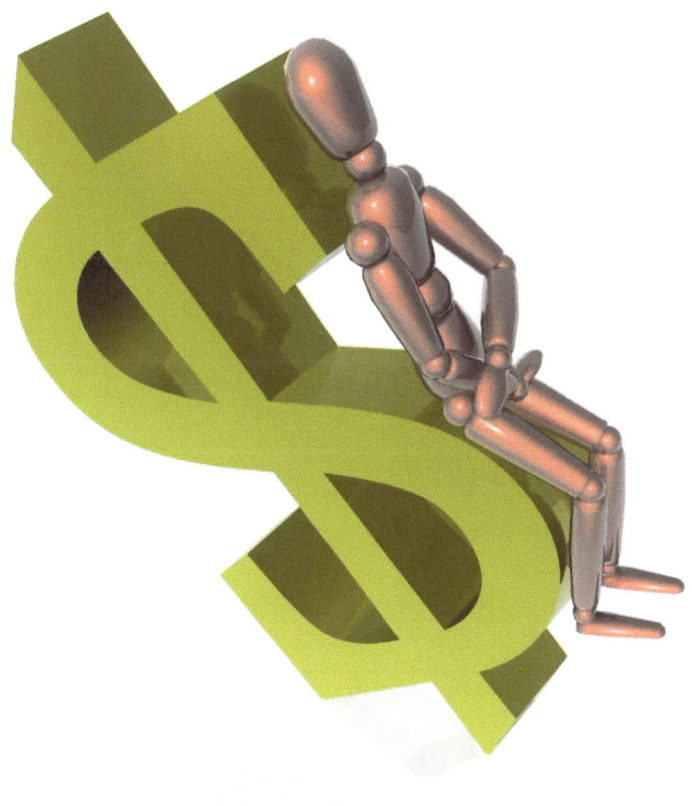

The Basics

There are three main types of affiliate marketers and these would include the full time marketer, the part-time marketer and the side-line marketer.

The full time marketer would probably depend heavily on the sole promotion of other businesses with revenue gained through the participation exercise.

The part-time marketer would employ affiliate programs as a major part of the business entity which in turn would create a significant percentage of their cumulated earnings. The side-line marketer would ideally only participate in promoting a very small number of companies.

This can vary but it would popularly be about two to three companies only. This in most cases would mean the promotion of their own web host to enable their cost to be adequately covered.

The time frame required to implement the respective affiliates would be rather minimal in comparison to other more complex internet tools but the results would be very impressive indeed.

Commonly placed on existing websites and most programs that have as copies, images and tracking links the affiliates are really quite easy to link to.

The most notable reason for adding affiliate to any online business endeavor lies in the revenue possibilities that could be very encouraging and lucrative.

The following are some popular affiliate networks:

- AffiliateFuel – these represent the major industries, with criteria that are very much stricter than commission junction.
- Click bank – primarily digital products which include downloading ebooks.
- Commission Junction – covers every major industry from travel to retail to many others.

Chapter 2:

Anticipate The Needs Of Your Market

Synopsis

In order to be able to take advantage of an affiliate program one needs to understand the varied needs of the market at the time the program is earmarked to be launched. These needs will play a pivotal role in deciding the corresponding affiliate that is most suited to be used.

What Do They Need

Categorizing affiliates into segments will allow the easier identification of what type of affiliates most suited to their needs. The categorizing exercise could be based on the primary promotional platform used and its subsequent adoptive style.

Using vouchers as an example the affiliated code tagged to this segment would be classifies as one separate type when comparisons are made to perhaps pricing categories.

Thus for the voucher code sites the visitor maybe looking for discount deals and clicking on the specific code will lead them to the information sought. Alternatively is the visitor was looking for better freebie deals then another code would be used to access these.

Different approaches should also be explored when deciding on the suitable affiliates. If the affiliates require content to be the prime reason for their search then the corresponding result will offer just that.

Affiliates are usually categorized by the promotional style content within the design of the site thus first understanding the site's contents will allow the choice of suitable affiliates to be made.

Sometimes using influential and established sources to create material endorsing something and then using that material as part of the affiliate category may also be useful.

It should be noted that presently there is a lot of circumstances where there is a great deal of crossovers between promotional efforts and the system or attraction element used within this promotion to generate the traffic to the sites thus the affiliates used will have both these features intertwined.

Chapter 3:
Supply Helpful Info About Affiliate Products You Promote

Synopsis

In order to be able to supply helpful information on the affiliate programs one is promoting one must first be able to keep the information of what is being offered concise and to the point.

Be Helpful

Offering this information based on matching the prospects' needs to what can be provided should ideally be the start of the whole exercise.

Designing simple yet descriptive bits of information to be used to tantalizing the prospect into making a commitment will be the successful way of creating helpful information.

Being able to anticipate if the information will be helpful is also another consideration that should be considered as if the information is deemed suitable it will be well accepted upon the recommendation.

The helpful information should ideally include the following points:

- Monitoring the sales data in terms of helpful information based on the buying and selling trends of the company and then introducing affiliates that describe in detail, programs that will help enhance the current situation should be well received.

- Providing information of affiliates that will enhance the edge over the competition will also be another platform to tap into. If the information on the affiliate is found to be helpful to the prospect then the committed participation is established.

- If the affiliate is predominantly promoting events such as trade shows on an international level then the relevant supporting data should be provided for the prospect to peruse. Information that is complimentary in fashion while showing the past exposure at such events and the affiliates advantages should be clearly outlined to ensure the affiliate programs is complete and promotable.

- Some affiliate programs provide information on what is current and if this is an instrumental advantage for the prospect then the program should be explained and promoted to them. Clearly outlining the benefits will help the prospect make an informed choice of the affiliate program offered.

Chapter 4:
Be Truthful With Your Customers And Subscribers

Synopsis

The first thing that I need to tell you right now, prior to us even looking at these techniques is to make 100% certain that the individuals signing up with you know what they are getting themselves into.

For instance, how many e-zines or newsletters have you ever subscribed to merely to find out that they're not in reality e-zines and newsletters, simply ad lists (which to be truthful aren't all that bad in certain situations).

Honesty

The decision you arrive at now will shape your business far in to the future, however more significantly whatever you tell your buyers and subscribers they will be receiving will shape your response rate substantially, and that is plainly something we will wish to take into account from the very beginning.

So there we have it. Principle number one, never tell your buyers they are getting something then refuse them that, or send them things that they have not called for or didn't know about, as not only will that get you into trouble, but it will as well affect the loyalty and trust these buyers and subscribers have with you, which is so crucial.

What we are aiming to establish here is a targeted and effective list that has response rates through the roof depending upon what you are promoting.

Do not forget this likewise includes affiliates, and might form a big part of your affiliate base.

You ought to be truthful to your buyers and be really careful with their personal details and not divulge it to any other 3rd party and you should likewise have regular communication with your subscribers.

Getting an autoresponder which will likewise keep you out of the anti - spam filter will likewise help you a lot.

Among the most crucial things that you should do is to get personal. You should address your subscribers by their name and keep your e-mails short and exact.

Although you may feel that you need to describe your products in detail, you ought to resist that temptation and not bore your buyers with lengthy e-mails and keep it as short as possible nevertheless conveying everything you wanted to in the first place.

Make it simple and inform your subscribers about the advantages that they get out of it.

Chapter 5:
Research Offers And Test Them First

Synopsis

There are several positive reasons why a product or business should be researched and tested for its credibility and impact before it reaches the stage where it is ready to be exposed to the customer or subscriber.

Check It Out

These advantages may include interaction between the products and market will be better addressed. This is especially recommended if comparisons needs to be made with already well established market entities.

Through the focus on the product and its reception from those it has been introduced to, some idea of its acceptability can be gauged and the necessary changes if any can be adequately addressed and made.

By the reactions and response attracted through the whole exercise, other complimenting exercises can then be implemented and carried out.

These may include advertising campaigns that can be designed to suit the main agenda, assisting software can be sourced for the various business monitoring platforms to be established, resources that may be needed for the intention of gaining recognition for the entity may be identifies and a host of other connective elements maybe is decided upon.

Offers that seem to receive lack luster attention can then be altered or redesigned to bring forth the best of the product for the prospects to be favorably attracted to them. The cost factor in doing all this important testing at the very onset of the business launching exercise will lead to a lot of eventual savings when the right path has been identified for the campaigns chosen.

Well designed evaluations that address all the possible concerns for both parties will yield results that can be instrumental is follow up decision and eventual perception of the entities involved.

Ideally the research and tests done should include various levels within the design phase; promotional ideas that are intended to bring the product to the prospects attention, pricing and any value added elements that are going to be tagged on.

Chapter 6:
Learn How To Be Patient

Synopsis

Timing is often an element that can prove to be surprisingly impactful of any aspect of a business endeavor. Timing is everything for something and important for most individuals intending to venture into the realm of uncertainly when it comes to going into business.

Great Info

Therefore exercising some level of patience would be very beneficial indeed and the following points should create the understanding that constitutes this train of thought:

- Understanding that any business venture will take time to garner the desired revenue impact or results is important. Expecting results to be forthcoming almost immediately can not only cause stress and concern it can also lead to a good style not being given the chance to prove itself before unnecessary changes are made. When there are too many changes too soon, the resulting effects will be confusing and frustrating to all parties.

- Being patient also means being actively involved in the exercise of consistency. Sitting back and simply allowing things to happen will also not be positively beneficial. Staying consistent until all possibilities are exhausted or until positive results are evident should be the tried and true methodology to follow from the very onset of any endeavor.

- Staying active does not in any way mean blindly doing things without any proper goal or dream firmly in place. It is very important to work towards a goal and breaking down the main goal into smaller and less daunting segments is recommended.

This will help on the journey toward keeping patient and striving towards the main end goal. This will take time and patience but is well worth the effort, energy and centered focus.

- Patience is also going to be the ingredient that keeps the individual from giving up when the going gets tough. When the element of patience is prevalent then the negativity of panic setting in can be effectively avoided.

Wrapping Up

Being able to use tools that can provide added revenue earning possibilities will help enormously in any business. This can be explored through the many affiliates that are currently available for use. These often lucrative ways of gaining added revenue can also contribute to the heightened awareness of the service, product or business being linked to the exercise of using the affiliates successfully.

Ideally a good affiliate marketer would be able to earn sales commissions each time clicks or purchases are made online. This of course has a phenomenally unbound amount of possibilities if the chosen affiliate is well managed and beneficial to the style of the site it is tagged to. Earnings can be made through subsidies in the form of a guarantee sale at the individual own featured site or from an affiliated merchant's site whenever there is an ongoing action of purchases of products, services, membership drives or programs on other websites too.

The latest and purportedly a highly successful way of gaining revenue through the affiliates are in the customer reciprocation affiliate. This is touted to be a competitive and fast growing way of earning revenue through customer acquisition exercises. There are also a whole host of other good affiliates that contribute handsomely to the revenue earning of those wisely utilizing this method of subsidized income.

Affiliate marketing is solely based on financial motivation to drive sales while other types may rely on other elements to compliment the business entity.

Individuals considering online businesses should also consider including affiliate marketing into the equation as in most cases it uses a pay for performance style whereby the individual does not necessarily incur any marketing expenses unless results are accrued. However though much encouraged it should be noted that affiliate offers are often not easy to select and manage without the corresponding tools of the trade available.